SPRINGS OF INSPIRATION

SPRINGS OF INSPIRATION

Compiled by **Michael James**

STANYAN BOOKS

RANDOM HOUSE

A Stanyan Book
Published by Stanyan Books,
8721 Sunset Blvd.,
Hollywood, California 90069
and by Random House, Inc.
201 East 50th Street,
New York, N.Y. 10022

Library of Congress Catalogue Card
Number: 73-8006
ISBN: 0-394-48595-5
Printed in U.S.A.

Designed by Hy Fujita
First Printing

Your life will be rich for others
only as it is rich for you.

— DAVID McCORD

The best way to know God is to
love many things.
— VINCENT VAN GOGH

Work as if you were to live 100 years;
pray as if you were to die tomorrow.
— BENJAMIN FRANKLIN

The only way in which you can attain
even moments of mental peace is
through the positive recognition of good.
— SAMMY DAVIS, JR.

Nothing more excites all that is
noble and generous than virtuous love.
— JOHN HOME

Happy is the man that findeth wisdom,
and the man that getteth understanding.
— PROVERBS, 3:13

There's a oneness about the earth from space that we can't see from the ground. We can't see any differences in national boundaries, we can't see any differences in colors or religion or political beliefs. They're nonexistent, if you sit back and look at earth as I did.

— ASTRONAUT ALFRED WORDEN

ED SIMPSON

Perish dark memories,
There's light ahead—
This world's for the living,
Not for the dead.
Down the great currents
Let the boat swing,
There was never winter
But brought the spring!

— KATHRYN MAYE

I cultivate peace at the center.
I'm a Quaker, you know. And if that
peace at the center is operative,
it absorbs blows and tensions.
— HERBERT HOOVER

The times are evil, but live nobly
and you will change the times.
— ST. AUGUSTINE

I beg leave to suggest to my well-fed
readers, those who have at their
command more victuals and drink than
they can possibly swallow; I beg to
suggest whether this would not be a
good way for them all to find the
means of bestowing charity?

You may give gifts without caring—
but you can't care without giving.

— FRANK A. CLARK

When there is room in the heart
there is room in the house.

— DANISH PROVERB

Gospel songs are the songs of hope.
When you sing gospel you have the
feeling there is a cure for what's wrong.

— MAHALIA JACKSON

The year's at the spring,
The day's at the morn
Morning's at seven
The hillside's dew-pearled.
The lark's on the wing
The snail's on the thorn,
God's in His heaven:
All's right with the world!

— ROBERT BROWNING

HY FUJITA

If you forgive people enough,
you belong to them and they to you,
whether either person likes it or not—
squatter's rights of the heart.

— JAMES HILTON

Faith has to do with things that are
not seen, and hope to do with things
that are not in hand.

— THOMAS AQUINAS

It is the mind that makes the body rich.

— WILLIAM SHAKESPEARE

It is only important to love the world . . .
to regard the world and ourselves
and all beings with love,
admiration and respect.

— HERMANN HESSE

Holiness is an infinite compassion
for others.

— SISTER THERESA KOPELL

Life is a sweet and joyful thing for one
who has someone to love and
a pure conscience.

— LEO TOLSTOY

I heard a bird sing
in the dark of December ...
A magical thing
and sweet to remember.

— OLIVER HERFORD

If God did not exist it would
be necessary to invent him.

— VOLTAIRE

The gloom of the world is but a shadow.
Behind it, yet within reach, is joy.
There is a radiance and glory in the
darkness, could we but see, and to see
we have only to look. I beseech
you to look.

— FRA GIOVANNI, 1513 A.D.

Prayer should be the key of the morning
and the lock of the night.

— OWEN FELLTHAM

If we are going to let our lights shine
simply to illumine our own faces,
we might as well let them go out.

— GEORGE GORDON

When I fail to cherish life in every fibre,
the fires within are waning.

— GEORGE MEREDITH

I'm an optimist. It does not seem
too much use being anything else.

— SIR WINSTON CHURCHILL

By night, an atheist half-believes a God.

— EDWARD YOUNG

A great man is one sentence.
History has no time for more than one
sentence, and it is always a
sentence that has an active verb.

— CLARE BOOTHE LUCE

I hold there ain't no use dyin' before
yer time. Lots of folk is walkin' round
jes' as dead as they ever will be.
I believe in gettin' as much good outen
life as you kin.

— ALICE HEGAN RICE
Mrs. Wiggs of the Cabbage Patch

I always prefer to believe the best of
everybody—it saves so much trouble.

— RUDYARD KIPLING

Trees are climbed from the bottom,
not from the top.

— FINNISH PROVERB

If you can find a path with no obstacles,
it probably doesn't lead anywhere.

— FRANK A. CLARK

Keep your face toward the sunshine
and the shadows will fall behind you.

— MICHAEL WHITMAN

I believe that man will not merely endure; he will prevail. He is immortal ... because he has a soul, a spirit capable of compassion and sacrifice and endurance.

— WILLIAM FAULKNER

In spite of all his cunning and
self-confidence, man is no better off in
this world than in a dark forest,
unless he has a Father in heaven Who
loves him with an eternal love,
and a Holy Spirit in heaven Who will
give him a right judgment
in all things, and a Saviour in heaven
Who can be touched with a feeling
of his infirmities.

— CHARLES KINGSLEY

The early morning hours symbolize for me a rebirth ... God has granted another day of life. He has granted another chance to do something good and worthwhile for humanity.

— DR. MICHAEL deBAKEY

How difficult it is to be wisely charitable
—to do good without multiplying
the source of evil. To give alms is
nothing unless you give thought also.
— JOHN RUSKIN

A time to embrace and a time to refrain
from embracing. A time to get and
a time to lose: a time to keep,
and a time to cast away.
— ECCLESIASTES

ED SIMPSON

One of the things we like best about
spring is that it comes just when
it's needed most.

— ARNOLD GLASGOW

Let grace and goodness be the principal
loadstone of thy affections. For love
which hath ends, will have an end;
whereas that which is founded on true
virtue, will always continue.

— JOHN DRYDEN

There is a land of the living and a land
of the dead and the bridge is love,
the only survival, the only meaning.

— THORNTON WILDER

The simple worship of love and
fertility can be immensely appealing
in a materialistic age overshadowed
by the achievements and horrors
of science.

— ALEX SANDERS

Love is the emblem of eternity:
it confounds all notion of time:
effaces all memory of a beginning,
all fear of an end.

— MME. de STAEL

If any man could rise to public office
and bring to that office the teachings
and precepts of the Prince of Peace,
he would revolutionize the world
and men would remember him for
a thousand years.

— BENJAMIN FRANKLIN

Life is so generous a giver, but we,
judging its gifts by their covering,
cast them away as ugly, or heavy
or hard. Remove the covering and you
will find beneath it a living splendor,
woven of love, by wisdom, with power.

— FRA GIOVANNI, 1513 A.D.

From an 18th century obituary:

She was
Liberal, without Prodigality
Frugal, without Parsimony
Cheerful, without Levity
Exalted, without Pride.
In person, Amiable
In conversation, Affable
In friendship, Faithful
Of Envy, void.

If we spend our lives in loving,
we have no leisure to complain
or to feel unhappiness.

— JOSEPH JOUBERT

We're not primarily put on this earth
to see through one another,
but to see one another through.

— PETER DE VRIES

Peace I leave with you, my peace I give
unto you; not as the world giveth,
give I unto you. Let not your heart be
troubled, neither let it be afraid.

—JOHN 14:27

Cherish all your happy moments;
they make a fine cushion for old age.

— BOOTH TARKINGTON

I sleep, I eat and drink, I read and
meditate, I walk in delightful fields . . .
And he that hath so many causes of
great joy is much in love with sorrow
who loses all these pleasures,
and chooses to sit down upon his little
handful of thorns.

— JEREMY TAYLOR

Eloquence is the transference of thought and emotion from one heart to another, no matter how it is done.

— JOHN B. GOUGH

Beloved, let us love so well,
Our work shall still be better
for our love,
And still our love be sweeter
for our work,
And both commended,
for the sake of each,
By all true workers and true
lovers born.

— ELIZABETH B. BROWNING

One of the good things that come of a
true marriage is that there is one face
which you can still see the same,
through all the shadows which years
have gathered upon it.

— GEORGE MACDONALD

Friendship is the comfort,
the inexpressible comfort of
feeling safe with a person.

— GEORGE ELIOT

The fool, with all his other faults,
has this also: he is always getting
ready to live.

— EPICURUS

As life is made up for the most part,
not of great occasions, but of small
everyday moments, it is the giving to
those moments, their greatest
amount of peace, pleasantness and
sincerity that contributes most to
the sum of human good.

— LEIGH HUNT

Do you believe in fairies?
If you do, clap your hands.

— JAMES BARRIE
Peter Pan

It is worth a thousand pounds sterling
a year to have the habit of looking
on the bright side of things.

— JEREMY BENTHAM

Nought endures but change.
— LUDWIG BOURNE

No one has completed his education
who has not learned to live with
an insoluble problem.
— EDMUND J. KIEFER

How strange to use "You only live once"
as an excuse to throw it away.
— BILL COPELAND

All that is necessary for the forces of
evil to win the world is for enough
good men to do nothing.
— EDMUND BURKE

We do not what we ought;
What we ought not, we do;
And lean upon the thought
That Chance will bring us through.
— MATTHEW ARNOLD

See that none render evil for evil unto
any man; but ever follow that which
is good, both among yourselves,
and to all men.

— I THESSALONIANS, 5:15

Never answer an angry word with an
angry word. It's the second one
that makes the quarrel.

— W. A. NANCE

Let us be patient, tender, wise, forgiving,
In this strange task of living;
For if we fail each other, each will be
Grey driftwood lapsing to the bitter sea.

— MARTIN ARMSTRONG

Prayer is and remains always
a native and deepest impulse
of the soul of man.

— THOMAS CARLYLE

I know the Bible is inspired, because it
finds me at greater depths of my
being than any other book.

— SAMUEL T. COLERIDGE

While the earth remaineth, seedtime
and harvest, and cold and heat,
and summer and winter, and day and
night shall not cease.

— GENESIS, 8:22

Let us therefore follow after the things
which make for peace . . .

— ROMANS, 14:19